ORDER OVER CHAOS

Cliff Green

Dedication

To My °
&
Loved
1111111111111111111111111111111111

Preface

Order Over Chaos builds on the life-changing ideas and concepts in my first book, *Less Than a Sack of Weed*. My goal with this book is to restore order to its proper place.

When I was putting this book together, I didn't intentionally balance it by starting it with my mother's wisdom and ending it with my father's. It landed like that as if it were divinely meant to be.

I hold the nuclear family in high regard, and anything that tries to break up the family intends to cause chaos. The man is the head of the household, and the woman is the nurturer who holds everything together.

Men bring order, and order comes with laws. Even if you disagree with my nuclear family statement, the chapter about Laying Down the Law applies to every man. But can the man be the head of his household if his lower head isn't working correctly? This book has the answer.

The people in my ° share similar values! My brother Pete turns excellent ideas into phenomenal 1s. He told me to switch this book's back cover with its front. Can we agree that this book's cover is like no other?

My brother Jason holds me accountable. He ensures that my words are followed by action. And when the goal is accomplished, he supports me like a real 1.

All my brothers keep each other ||||| (in line). There's order amongst us because we don't allow chaos in our °. We know that chaos creates confusion. Our foundation is solid, and yours will be, too, when you learn to let go of so & so. This book will tell you how to keep your circle small.

With every ounce of love, dedication, and determination in my heart to make this world a better place, I bring you Order Over Chaos!

Table of Contents

"Don't Talk To Strangers!" – Robin Green

I love my mom, and I am grateful for her instructions. My mom dropped a jewel when she told me not to talk to strangers. She knew a stranger couldn't be trusted. She is why I don't trust, admire, or adorn people I've only seen on TV.

Anyone I haven't looked in the eyes is a stranger. I don't know them or the content of their character. How could I trust someone I never met?

While watching TV, we are bombarded with subliminal messages. All subliminal messages do not have to be malicious. But, if we're honest, it's clear that most of the messages on TV are wicked.

Subliminal messages can make people do things they may have never considered doing. They secretly implant ideas into our minds. Buried deep within our minds are thoughts that aren't original.

In my first book, *Less Than a Sack of Weed*, I wrote about how our thoughts become reality. The book you are reading at this moment wasn't always here. I thought about these ideas before I put them on paper.

People in high places control the media. These same people know that thoughts manifest into reality. The media has been used to degenerate our thoughts.

There aren't many wholesome shows on TV anymore. There are some animal channels, real estate shows, and cooking shows that aren't bad. But how many other shows promote righteous lifestyles?

1

Everything on TV is about drugs, death, murder, adultery, and gluttony.

When I figured this out, I stopped watching TV. I'm careful of what I let enter my mind.

It's not hard to create a subliminal message. I put one in the picture of a blog post. The time displayed on the clock was 11:30. While looking at the picture, you may have thought that 11:30 was the time I took the photo.

Nope, it represented the day I arrived on earth. What if I made the message a little more subtle? I could make you think 11:30 or 11/30 is significant. It's important to me but not necessarily to you.

Therein lies the danger of trusting the characters you see on TV. Actors are the faces you see. At least you can see their faces. But they are playing a role written by someone you rarely see or know.

If I can put a subliminal message in the picture, think of the messages that some of these writers and producers may be putting into the shows you and your family watch.

Remember that these people in high places seem to want to push chaos. To stop the degeneracy from entering your mind, please scale back from watching TV. This will minimize the number of subliminal messages entering your mind.

Your mind will be free. You will be able to think clearly and develop original thoughts. Your creativity and imagination will return to the level of childhood.

The void you've been feeling will become whole. No one wants to feel like everything around them is in shambles. Turning off your TV will bring order to your life.

I am also willing to bet your mom told you not to talk to strangers. So please don't take my word for it; listen to your mom's advice. Moms always seem to know best!

Art

As mentioned in the previous chapter, I don't watch TV. The moment I cut TV out of my life was when my life became full of color.

The picture that I painted for my life became my reality. I always dreamed of getting paid to travel, and now I do.

I've always been inclined to help people, and now I write books to do just that. I also make health and wellness videos to motivate others, hand-crafted jewelry, and recently started a clothing line based on my motto: "**GO HARD OR DIE EASY ®**[1]."

I started coloring, drawing, and painting again. I own the home I grew up in. I find time to take care of my health. I'm also able to spend time with my family and loved ones.

When people ask me how I find the time to do so much, I tell them I don't watch others go after and live their dreams. I focus on doing the things that I love to do.

Please grab my first book and read the chapter EXPRESS Yourself.[2] I explained how art is used to mold our perspective.

Not too long ago, my nephew, Zy'en, told me he wanted more art classes in school. Sadly, schools

---

[1] Green, Cliff. "Go Hard or Die Easy." *Less Than a Sack of Weed,* 2020, pp 39 - 41

[2] Green, Cliff. "EXPRESS Yourself." *Less Than a Sack of Weed*, 2020, pp 47 - 48

nationwide have been removing their art programs from their curriculums.

Our duty as parents and concerned citizens is to keep the arts alive. Our houses should have an artistic corner or art studio for our children. A corner that will foster their imagination.

Art is powerful. Art moves people. Art is more than paintings hanging on walls. Art is a lifestyle. Art is an expression of self. With this book, I aim to give your mind a clean canvas. To cut the *chaos* and bring *order* to your world.

You will see the power you have within. You will express yourself to the fullest. I want you to paint a bright picture of your life.

Please draw, write, and highlight these pages as you read along. This will help you remember the messages. Be artistic in everything you do. A chaotic thought expressed through art can turn into millions of dollars.

Have you ever walked through a museum and asked why a crazy-looking painting was hanging on the wall? Someone may have painted what they have seen as chaos and turned it into a fortune!

You have the power to do the same!

Please Back Up & Chill!

Chaos is everywhere. I notice chaotic behavior every time I get behind the wheel. I get annoyed when people drive too close to the person in front of them.

Back up! Give yourself some time to maneuver if something unexpected happens. Don't put yourself in a situation where you're reactive instead of proactive.

Plus, you can't force the person in front of you to speed up or switch lanes. It's smarter to change lanes and go around that person. Voila, that's the end of that problem.

Let's examine what could go wrong while trailing someone. The person in front of you can slam on the brakes and cause you to hit them. The person who rear-ends someone is always at fault.

Suppose you do rear-end someone. You may be injured from the incident. Now you have hospital bills. You will have to go to court. Now you have legal fees. The car needs to be fixed. Now you have repair costs or a new car note. This would've been avoided had you backed up and chilled!

Be mindful of other people's situations. Maybe the person in front of you isn't speeding because they have children in the car. Perhaps they value life. Maybe they're not rushing because they see the foolishness in speeding.

Whatever it is, fall back, take your time, and cruise. This applies to more than driving. It applies to life. Relax and enjoy the scenery.

Please back up and chill!

P.S. Please stay out of the left lane if you're not passing by. Learn the unwritten laws of the road. Thank you!

So & So

Learn to watch the company you keep. Especially if you have goals you're focused on.

Watch out for so & so. So & so is a good person, but so & so likes to do things that aren't aligned with your goals. If you let so & so into your life, they will knock you off track.

Your logic tells you not to chill with them, but your ego reminds you of all the good times you've had together. You end up chilling with so & so in search of those good feelings. That temporary feeling feels good, but it's dangerous. It can pull you back into a life you have claimed to give up.

We all know how it goes: "After today, I'm done! No more! I'm buckling down and getting serious!" You meant it that time, but you're scared. You're afraid of how people will perceive you for changing.

You know so & so doesn't want to see you take steps to improve. When they see you improve, they will have to follow suit or attempt to keep you where you once were. You've heard it from so & so's mouth before: "Oh, you changed! You aren't the same anymore!"

You let the fear of what people may or may not think about you hold you back. It cripples you from growing and becoming the person you aim to become.

Live without fear. Be who you truly are! If you strive to reach new levels in life, be that person. If you're okay with being complacent and stuck in the same monotonous cycle, be that person. But if you are complacent, learn to let go of the people who seek to do better. Never shun them for doing so.

Learn to let people go. Don't worry about what other people may think of you. Even if they look at you funny, that's fine. In the end, you're winning!

I've had plenty of so & sos in my life. I let many of them go. Hopefully, my journey to become my best will help them to become their best.

Always strive to do your best. Never let small-minded people stop you from reaching the stars where you belong.

All Isn't Lost

I was riding through my old neighborhood, and as usual, I was paying attention to the empty lots and abandoned houses. Lowkey, I was getting depressed. Sometimes, it feels like I am the only one who can see what's happening. At times, it feels like no one even cares.

I have taken a rake and broom and cleaned up the block or walked down the street to clean up a lot. I hate returning a few days later to see it in such a lousy state. It makes me feel like all my work was for nothing.

One lot about half a block from my house was killing me for quite some time. I tried to clean it up before, but the trash was too much to handle, so it piled back up.

When I rode past it earlier that day, I was thinking about ways that I could clean it up, but then I asked myself, "Why do I continue to clean up after people who don't care about themselves or their environment?"

The thought of giving up crossed my mind until I was driving back up the street later that day when I noticed a lady with a rake and a young man with a shovel in his hands. I pulled up to my house, got out of the car, and looked down the street. To my surprise, they were walking over to the same lot.

I walked down the street to see what was up. And to my surprise, they were about to clean up the lot! Wow! God throws curveballs at you! God was showing me that all isn't lost. There are people out here putting in work.

I had to introduce myself to them! As we talked, I told them I felt like giving up until I saw them and that they reflected that fire inside me.

The conversation was even better because they were both privy to deep knowledge. The young man was only 15 but wise beyond his years. It's rare to meet a young man who is aware of the problems the world is facing. This showed me that good parenting and giving your child direction while young will go a long way.

We talked for a while, and then I exchanged my information with them and told them I would be willing to help the next time I came to town.

The moral of this story is that all isn't lost. Some people genuinely care, even though finding them is like finding a needle in a haystack. They are out here! When you see them, please take a second or two to let them know that you are also working to bring the order back. They may have been feeling like I initially was.

That is how we will build a better world. Never lose hope!

Order Starts At Home

I have witnessed many things growing up in my community. I write this with all the conviction in my heart. We must be honest with ourselves and others, or we will never progress.

I do not aim to exclude other nationalities but to have them read, learn, and help where they see fit. Please do not be offended or defensive about what you are about to read.

There have been many inhumane things that happened to Black men and women in America that have led to the destruction of our neighborhoods. Understanding and learning from our history will make a brighter future.

It would be wise to understand that one nationality's progression does not mean another's regression. If we were wise enough to move in unison, the progression of one would be the progression of everyone.

We haven't been honest about why we are still in the situation that we are in. The truth of the matter is that Black people have been running from the truth for some time.

Once you hear and understand the truth, you have a couple of choices. You can A) hear and abide by it, or B) completely ignore it and keep doing what you were comfortable doing for so long.

Let me give you an example. I was reading through the YouTube comments of a guy in the Black community. This guy made some money and moved to an affluent neighborhood. Many people were mad at him and called him a fraud. I don't know this man personally, so I have no say in what he is or isn't.

Some of the comments were saying things like, "He should've stayed in the hood. He drives all these cars. He could be using his money to build schools for us."

Those comments made me think, "Aren't schools already in our neighborhoods?" Yes, there are schools in our communities. And yes, these schools don't teach us everything we need to know. I know that we have to build our own. But let's get back to being honest and truthful.

Black people do NOT care, especially about school. I know that people will be mad at that statement, and my stance may evolve into something different because people change with growth. But if I were to call it as I see it, Black youth do not care about school.

I am Black and went to a predominantly Black school in what most people would call the "Hood." I remember how we acted in school from my own experience. I'm embarrassed as I sit here and recollect some memories of what we did. The truth is, we were terrible.

Let's look at a few things that we did. Everybody talked endlessly and never shut up, even when the teacher asked us to. Our utter disrespect for our school's property, especially the books, is mind-boggling. We disrespected teachers and other authoritative figures.

Even though we lived in the hood and were all broke, we were always worried about who wore the latest shoes or outfits. The list can go on and on, but you get the picture.

I witnessed this firsthand as a student and as a youth program counselor. It is the same thing today as it was when I was in school.

If we want to fix or heal our situation, everyone, especially parents, must be honest with themselves and take responsibility for their children's behavior. Even though schools may not teach us true history, they still teach two fundamental things we need to prosper: math and science.

No matter your complexion, excelling in those two subjects will lead to success. I know we would like to blame the schools, and I am not deflecting that blame because they still bear a lot of it, but let's look at this situation more deeply.

MOST teachers didn't become teachers searching for the glamorous, high-paying career it would give them. They became teachers because they had a passion for it. They loved the idea of positively changing a child's life.

It's just like with anything else: if you keep trying to do what you love and all you get in return is rotten apples, sooner or later, your passion will dwindle.

Of course, some Black youth care and want to excel academically. How does that saying go? Does one bad apple ruin the bunch? And there are a lot of bad apples.

So, how are you raising your children? Are they academically inclined or television-inclined? Are you teaching them behavior that has them protesting in the classroom, or are you teaching them to be pro-test? Are you teaching them to be leaders or to be followers? Are your kids more inclined to remember music lyrics or their algebra lessons?

Be honest with yourself. How is your parenting style? Don't be offended by these questions. If you want to reverse the ills in our neighborhoods, the real work starts at home.

I know I will get flack for this from somebody who didn't read it with a logical mind, but I'm not scared of the truth. I stand on it! I pray that you do as well.

The order starts at home!

You Have The Right To Remain Silent

Talk less, do more!

This is one of the hardest things to do because people always question us and pry for information. I hate to bring this negative to the light, but some people do not like seeing others shine. When they see a person's light shining, they get hit with a jealous bug and want to pry into that person's life.

These people ask as many questions as possible and carefully analyze every answer they hear, looking for a flaw. We are all imperfectly perfect beings with flaws that naturally come out when speaking.

While answering all the questions we naively take as another person's curiosity, we add fuel to a fire we didn't know existed. This person is looking for our flaws so that they can point them out as an aha moment when we make a mistake or don't accomplish what we said we would. It's not that we didn't achieve our objective. It just didn't happen in the timeframe that person thought it should.

It's kind of sad for real, but we live in a society of hardened hearts[3]. People should use their energy to correct and improve the situation. But they would rather hold your error as an "*I got you*" thing. It's as if they're thinking, "Even though they are doing so much, I knew they couldn't really be doing all that stuff!" It's as if they

---

[3] Green, Cliff. "Hardened Hearts." *Less Than a Sack of Weed*, 2020, pp 21 - 24

need to know that you have messed up and will mess up in the future for them to feel good about themself.

I don't want to paint the wrong picture. Not everyone has bad intentions. Some people genuinely care about you and want to see you reach your full potential.

But to dead the negative people, the best thing to do is to be quiet. Please don't speak about your goals until they are planned and you have taken steps to implement them.

Proverbs 21:23 says, "He who guards his mouth and his tongue keeps himself from calamity." Proverbs 17:28 reads, "Even a fool is thought wise if he keeps silent, and discerning if he holds his tongue." In the absence of words, you are less likely to say something foolish or something that can be used against you.

Police inadvertently drop a jewel when they tell us we have the right to remain silent. Use your right to remain silent in all situations. For most of us, silence is awkward. That awkward feeling shows that we lack discipline in taming our tongues. I am guilty of this.

Don't always be the first person to say something. Learn to read people by what they say, then determine if they are there to help progress you forward or if they are energy vampires. If they are vampires, remember that vampires can't stand the light. So, continue to shine by being a person of action because actions speak louder than words.

Talk less, do more!

You Only Have One Body

Your health is your responsibility, not anyone else's. God has given you a mind and a body for you to use. You're the only person who can feel what is wrong with your body. Those pains, illnesses, and diseases are ways your body communicates to tell you something is wrong.

A doctor will only tell you what you already know, then prescribe something to mask the problem but not heal it.

Doctors don't get paid when people are healthy. I am not implying that all doctors have evil intent, but unhealthy people keep their paychecks coming, at least with Western medicine.

A lot of these doctors give patients negative news. The negative news puts their patient in a negative emotional and mental state. Those negative feelings exasperate the problem.

Think about when they give a person a time frame on how long that person has left to live. Once a person hears that time frame, they will continually and constantly think about it until their thoughts manifest into reality and, ultimately, their untimely death.

The best thing you can do is heal yourself. Lose the weight you need to lose by exercising more. Join a yoga or Pilates class. Get a personal trainer if you must. Get a juicer or a good blender and put it to work twice a day, thrice if you're focused. Cleanse your system of the everyday toxins that you eat and intake.

Learn how to breathe deep to heal your lungs and bring oxygen back into your system. Go for walks in the park, where trees cleanse the air. Research the importance of the sun and how to gaze at it properly.

Quit eating junk food. I am not talking about that delight you must indulge in occasionally- we all have those- I know I do. I am talking to the people who consistently eat junk food and then wonder why they get junk results. Again, God has given us brains to use. Don't continually ingest it if you know it isn't good for you.

Consequences result from doing the opposite of what you knew you were supposed to do. We reap what we sow. Also, intentionally doing what you know you shouldn't is a direct slap to God's face.

Please start caring for your health before it is too late. You only have this one body and brain. You can use it or lose it!

Where's Your Money?

I can't remember the song's title, but I remember what the artist said. He said something like, "I have so many millions. I go to the teller and take something out, and don't worry about the amount of money in the account."

He was insinuating that he has so much money that he doesn't keep track of what he has or doesn't care to keep track of his amount. I get it. That's what rappers do. They like to stunt and flash money.

I want these young men to get all the money they can. I also want them to add financial literacy to their lyrics because young people are listening and are being led astray. Whether rappers know it or even care to know it, they have so much influence on our youth.

The consistent message in mainstream rap is about how rappers can blow 40 bands in the club in just one night. That's cool, and I'm glad you're getting to the bag. But can we change the narrative?

I know many help their families, friends, and loved ones; some even help their community. But that's not what's heard or seen.

You aren't supposed to do your good deeds for recognition, but can we discuss the positive things more often? Can we talk about how you put one of your best boys or family members through college to obtain a degree in accounting or business management so that they can manage you and your money?

Do you enjoy leaving your money in the hands of people you don't trust? People who may not have your best interest at heart. That statement can be made for athletes as well.

These lyrics promote financial illiteracy as if it's cool. Let's look at how economic ignorance is dangerous. What if you went into the bank one day to withdraw funds, and the teller told you that you had an amount in your account that was way less than what you thought you had?

You try to dispute the situation with the teller but have been living financially irresponsibly. Chances are you will lose this dispute and whatever money you *thought* you had but didn't *know* for sure.

You would be angry, and the rest of the week would be messed up. To avoid a situation like this, the best thing to do is keep all your bank and shopping receipts. Receipts record where you've been spending your money.

Plus, certain purchases can be written off on your taxes at the end of the year. It's easy to do. You only need an envelope or a shoebox to put your receipts in. And voila, you are now getting your finances in order.

Another thing I have noticed from all my street homies is that they need to carry their money better. They stuff it into their pockets any and every way. They put it in different pockets. It usually falls out when they go into their pocket to pull out their phone or whatever they need.

We have to bring order to our finances. Why do we work so hard to get the money to turn around and lose the money?

Learn to organize your cash. Get a wallet, money clip, or even a rubber band to hold your cash. Keep track of your money. Know how much money you have on you, along with how much you have in your bank account. Take control of your finances.

Make a budget and checklist of your necessities. For example:
- Mortgage or rent
- Utility bills
- Car note, insurance, and gas
- Food for the week or month
- Phone bill
- Credit card bill
- School loans
- Miscellaneous

Many people on the internet give away free knowledge on how to keep and grow your money.

Financial burdens bring stress and chaotic feelings. Having order over your finances will get rid of the chaos.

Please don't wait until it's too late. Write a list now. Do it on the inside cover of this book if you must. Inflation is at an all-time high. Now is the best time to take back control of your finances.

Raising Kids In Today's World

Kids are pure, untainted, and free from all the ills plaguing society. They come into this world with a clean slate. They are filled with love, joy, peace, and happiness. They laugh. They cry. They play. Kids are curious beings with imaginations unfathomable to the average adult.

I hate to see beautiful children with all the potential in the world being neglected by their parents. It saddens me. But as the days go on, I've noticed it more and more. I've seen parents hollering and cursing at their children with malice.

I've witnessed kids trying to get their mother's attention, but the mother was too busy listening to music to notice. What's even worse is when parents play that trash music around their children, unaware that their children are soaking up every message in those songs.

If you have kids or are around kids, are you doing everything you tell them not to do? For instance, my friend smokes cigarettes around his son. He better believe that his little man is watching him and that he will emulate what he has seen his dad do.

If his son starts to smoke one day, how could my friend tell him that he shouldn't? Even if he lists all the adverse effects of tobacco to his son, his son will look at him and ask, "If you know all of that, then why do you smoke?"

The ills that plague the parent are passed on to the next generation. I used cigarette smoking as an example, but there are many more. As I stated earlier, kids come into the world with a clean slate and no hate in their hearts. It is a learned behavior that they get from their parents and the people they are around.

If we want our kids to be great, we must be great ourselves. Our children are watching[4] and analyzing everything we do. We must look within ourselves to see if these ills are deep in our minds and hearts. If so, do we portray them to the world? Because our children are watching and looking at us as examples.

What image are you portraying to your kids? Do you want your kids to be like you or better? We can't expect order from them if all we do is display chaos!

---

[4] Green, Cliff. "Somebody's Watching." *Less Than a Sack of Weed*, 2020, pp 6 - 8

Never Forget

The most advanced form of technology is the human brain. Our brain is the original supercomputer. It can record and keep track of everything that has happened to us.

Today's world has our minds continuously searching for instant gratification. The average attention span is the size of a fruit fly. Therefore, it is up to you to record your story, or it will forever be forgotten.

Most people have oral and written traditions that pass down their history to the next generation. In today's world, technology is wiping out these traditions.

There was a time when people gathered around as a community and listened to the stories of an elder. Some of their stories were so animated that listening to them would put watching movies or television to shame.

Come to think of it. We still have storytellers. Rappers are storytellers. Though it seems as if many of their stories are negative, you can see what they are saying while listening to them.

Storytellers were more than entertainers. They were teachers. They used stories to relay codes and messages that gave their audiences a deeper understanding of life.

The allegories and metaphors used made their listeners wiser. After listening to an elder's story, the crowd would leave with a more profound sense of self.

There was a time when I felt caught up in social media. Fortunately, after some self-reflection, I caught myself. I remember asking myself if I was addicted to my phone. Could I live without it?

A few days ago, I was listening (more like eavesdropping) to people speaking about their families' history, and it was astounding to me how in-depth they could go.

They talked about how their great-great-grandparents journeyed to the States. They told stories about their grandparents' lives and shared the exciting things their forefathers did.

I sat and thought about how much I didn't know about my family's history. It made me realize how much more work I must put into healing myself. To heal, I need to know my ancestral history. How could I claim to know myself but not know anything about my ancestry? What am I doing to keep my story[5] alive?

A person who has healed themselves will be more adept at healing others. Knowing world history is great, but knowing where your bloodline ascended is even better.

I can speak about world history but don't know my family tree. That is a problem for anyone in the same position.

We need our elders to start sharing their stories with us again. We need to know all their trials and tribulations.

Our elders' stories must be heard. Some elders may be unable to write, so I thought of a solution. This

[5] Green, Cliff. "Mystery – My Story – Mastery." *Less Than a Sack of Weed*, 2020, pp 64 - 65

only works if you are interested in learning your family's history. Next time you speak to an elder, ask them if they mind you recording the conversation. You can record it, then write it for them, or you can record it and turn the clips into a podcast.

We must write and record our stories to ensure that future generations know their history and are wise enough never to repeat it!

When Opportunity Knocks

Not too long ago, my friend confronted me about my intellectual capabilities. He told me that I was intelligent but not a genius.

I begged to differ but understood where he came from. He told me the only difference between myself and those around me is that I applied myself! He broke down different ways I applied myself over the years to get to where I am today. Then, it all made sense.

Most things in our lives happen to us by our own doing! My success took time to happen. It happened after years of staying focused on my goals. I was consistently working towards my goals until an opportunity arose.

When that opportunity arose, I took it and never looked back. I also did not let the fear of the unknown keep me from taking chances.

In *Less Than a Sack of Weed,* in the chapter *Don't Let Father Time Catch You Slipping*[6], I wrote about fear and how it is one of the most crippling things in our lives. I posed this question: Why do we fear things that haven't happened?

When opportunity knocks, open the door. Don't allow fear to stop you. Have faith in yourself and the capabilities that our Creator has instilled in you.

---

[6] Green, Cliff. "Don't let Father Time Catch You Slipping." *Less Than a Sack of Weed,* 2020, pp 42 - 43

Opportunity is all around you. Please take advantage of it!

Who Are You Going To Call?

Idolatry is at an all-time high. People are more concerned with actors and entertainers than their own families. People idolize entertainers. There isn't anything wrong with being an entertainer. But entertainment has been used since the beginning to keep the masses (us) from focusing on things that truly matter!

I heard a speech from an actor that people were raving about. There was no shade towards him because it was a good speech. But I'm guessing that since someone on TV said what we've been saying for years, people finally wanted to acknowledge it. It didn't matter when their friend told them the same thing.

I heard people screaming that we need to support Black-owned businesses and do this Black and that Black. I agree with those statements. But when the people you know have companies, are you supporting them?

How can we expect to build wealth with one another if we can't share the wealth with people we know? We are too caught up worrying about people we have never met on TV instead of worrying about the people who truly matter.

Think about it. When you needed that helping hand, who did you call? Your friend, family, loved one, or the person on TV? I'm just asking for clarification.

Who's Who?

Is there a code among people in the up community? By up community, I mean the people in the know—those who know what's happening in their communities and worldwide.

Because if there is a code, I need to know it! I live in the District of Columbia. A city labeled Chocolate City due to the high population of Black people living here. Since many Black people are around, I figured I would run into socially aware people all the time, but that hasn't been the case.

I love to be around and converse with "conscious" people. But where are they? I know they're out there. I met some incredible people while I was blogging. But on my day-to-day journey, I feel alone in this boat.

As a philosopher, I have a legitimate theory about why it is hard to meet good people. Many people, even socially aware people, are caught up in the illusion that the media has portrayed every Black person as evil.

We are so caught up that we tend not to trust or show love to anyone we do not know because they could be the next suspect in our minds. I know this to be true because I have fallen for the trap.

I'll give an example of how the media has persuaded us to think this way. For instance, if I was walking down the street behind you, and you didn't know me or what I was about, you wouldn't trust me. Even though I don't mean any harm, since the media portrays

Black people as evil and nasty, it makes you uneasy knowing a Black man is behind you.

This goes on and on for all your encounters with Black people. Most people are minding their business and trying to be their best. But we are all evil to you and everybody else who believes what the media has been portraying for decades.

I am not saying that these thoughts constantly fill your mind, but they do cross it. I am trying to get you to see who imprinted that thought on you in the first place. This psychological bondage is what we battle.

It doesn't just affect Black people. It affects how every other race views us as well. It affects their minds harder than ours because most of their knowledge of us comes from TV. I have had conversations that made me think, "Dang! This person believes everything he sees on TV."

It is time for us to wake up from this trance that the idiot box (TV) has us stuck in. Judge every man on the content of his character, not some made-up belief imposed on us.

As stated in The Sidewalk Law[7], I look at every man or woman I pass in the eye, followed by a nod or a simple hello. We don't live by the same code if it is not reciprocated.

---

[7] Green, Cliff. "The Sidewalk Law." *Less Than a Sack of Weed*, 2020, pp 52 - 54

Technology Isn't A Babysitter!

A few years back, while living with my uncle, one of my tasks was to watch my little cousin. I remember watching him play his game and thinking, "This kid is literally in another world."

I was sitting there watching him physically play the game, but mentally, he was in another world. He was playing a first-person shooter game that puts the player in the action on the front line of war.

Mentally, though he is unaware of it, my cousin's mind was in Ghana, killing Ghanaian people. It struck me as odd when I noticed that he was killing Africans. I asked myself if these games were a way to make people subconsciously become familiar with killing people.

The story gets crazier. Since the game can be connected to the internet, and that is how most people play games these days. He was playing the game with men and women from across the world. Did I mention that the game has a headset that allows players to talk to one another?

This eleven-year-old child was playing with and talking to adults through the headset. If that isn't a creep's dream, I don't know what is. Plus, the amount of foul language during these gaming stints is crazy.

If you were to listen to what your child has been listening to one day, you wouldn't even allow your kids to play these games.

As the title of this chapter says, Technology *isn't* your babysitter! Many parents like to sit back and let their kids watch TV. You may think that if they are watching cartoons, everything is okay. Because, hey, nothing can be wrong with cartoons.

If you were to do a simple YouTube search of subliminal messages in cartoons, thousands of results would pop up. Unbeknownst to most, cartoons promote wicked behavior. And have you ever considered who writes them?

It's not like kids are writing and drawing these cartoons for entertainment. It is grown adults writing these cartoons. A lot of cartoons are filled with adult messages. You may think your child didn't pick up the message, but our brains are the original supercomputers. Everything that goes into our minds is being stored.

I couldn't leave out the cell phone as the new babysitter. I don't even want to discuss this subject. Can I say, "STOP IT!"

Letting your kid stare at a screen for hours is terrible not only for their imagination but also for their eyes. For those who purchased this book as an eBook (I am grateful for your support), even if you read this on your laptop, tablet, phone, or computer screen, they're all terrible for your eyes. They are all artificial light.

Staring so close to something all day will weaken your eyes' ability to see long distances. There is a reason why the Dogon can see every star, planet, and constellation in the universe with nothing more than their God-given eyesight. They do not indulge in technology all day long.

Please don't read this and disregard it. Because if you are a parent, it's a monkey-see-monkey-do world. Your kids will emulate what they see you doing. Are you constantly glued to the phone, tablet, or computer screen? If it's terrible for our kids' eyes, it's also awful for us.

In Family Equals Perfection[8], I wrote that you are your child's god. Your child will imitate and do what they see you doing. I am not trying to tell you what to do, but I am telling you what to do. Go outside more. Read more books to your kids. Make reading a natural, fun part of their day.

When we were children, we didn't come into the house unless the temperature was *extremely* hot or cold. Video games were our last resort for having fun. We didn't have cell phones to play on 24/7, either. We used our imaginations. Please don't let your child grow up without imagination.

---

[8] Green, Cliff. "Family Equals Perfection." *Less Than a Sack of Weed*, 2020, pp 96 - 99

Tomorrow Never Comes

Tomorrow never comes! Think about that for a second. What did you think? Am I a quack, or is this a profound truth? It all depends on how you look at it.

We say things that make us believe there is a tomorrow, but one of the most famous quotes states, "Tomorrow isn't guaranteed!" That quote is a misnomer. It should read the same as the title of this chapter. Because Tomorrow Never Comes!

Let me break it down with a question that will hopefully make this make sense. Are you reading this now or tomorrow? Seriously, think about what I am asking you! Even if you say that you will read this tomorrow, wouldn't the moment you read this be your NOW? Tomorrow never came.

You can only be in the present moment. This isn't for people who have reached that god-consciousness and can project themselves into the future, but this will help everyone else get there.

Tomorrow, or the idea of tomorrow, is to get you to not live in the present. Tomorrow will have you not cherishing, loving, enjoying, and working to the best of your abilities now! This is not to say that you shouldn't plan for your future because I am an avid advocate of the power of writing down and organizing your objectives.

If you haven't read it already, I would advise you to read my first book, Less Than a Sack of Weed. There are many gems about the power of writing and planning, especially in the chapter "ORGANIZATION[9]."

I am living out and able to do everything I ever imagined I would because I have learned to take advantage of the present moment.

People live their dream lives because they have learned to maximize their time. I hope I have inspired you to do the same.

Because Tomorrow Never Comes!

[9] Green, Cliff. "ORGANIZATION." *Less Than a Sack of Weed*, 2020, pp 91 - 92

Dedication & Determination

To truly be dedicated to something, you must devote your time, energy, and effort to the task. The people we view as successful devote their lives to accomplishing their goals.

Dedication and determination are hard roads to travel. On your path, many roadblocks and obstacles will try to prevent you from accomplishing your goals. Just know that nothing in life comes easy.

Remember the motto: Go Hard or Die Easy.[10]

If obtaining success were easy, everybody would be successful. However, the things that are worth attaining come with hard work, dedication, and determination.

A determined mind can accomplish anything. If you can conceive it, you can achieve it. It sounds corny and cliché, but it's true.

After you conceive a brilliant idea, you must visualize it and devise a plan of attack. You can only see your entire plan if you keep your mind focused on your plan.

I have said this before and will repeat it a thousand times until more people understand: quit watching TV. I say that with all sincerity. I am not just saying it because it sounds good. It works.

---

[10] Green, Cliff. "Go Hard or Die Easy." *Less Than a Sack of Weed*, pp 40 - 42

I haven't watched television in over ten years and have accomplished almost everything I set out to accomplish. My goal list is still growing.

Think about this for a second: every person you see on TV has accomplished their goal of being on TV.

Not to offend the men who claim only to watch sports, but you're watching other men get money, fame, and power. You could be working towards getting the same things.

Instead of watching TV, you could be accomplishing your dreams, goals, and aspirations. After you achieve your goals, you will have the time and resources to attend as many games as you would like.

Don't get me wrong. I am all for people doing what they like because I will go to a game. The difference is that I sacrificed my time and energy to afford to do the things I wanted.

It's disheartening when people talk about their financial problems, weight issues, or even boredom when there is so much time in the day to go out and do something productive.

For my social media addicts, why are you scrolling through a timeline when you don't have your life in order? I'll let you think about that for a minute.

Everybody should detox themselves from social media. Use that time to clear your mind. Unless social media is helping you to advance your business, please stay away from it for some time. Social media is a deterrent and a time waster.

When I got back on social media, I started **www.cliffgr33n.com.** If it weren't for the site, I wouldn't have any. Low-key, you shouldn't either! It would be wise to dedicate your time to accomplishing your mission.

When you are dedicated and determined, you will do what you must, even when you don't feel like doing it. In doing so, you will develop new and better habits, leading you to the life you want to live.

Ask yourself, "Am I dedicated and determined?"

I'm A Free Man

Regarding school loans, you can have one big loan from one bank, many from the same bank, or several different banks. I had several (about ten), all from the same bank.

I had accumulated a lot of money from grinding, hustling, sacrificing, dedicating, and keeping my eyes on my goals. I had enough to repay my loans in one fell swoop. I contemplated whether I should for months.

Ask any of my friends. I would not keep my mouth closed when it came to these loans. I felt like they were such a burden weighing me down. However, I didn't tell anybody how much money I had because I didn't want them watching my pockets. But I sure was asking everybody how they would pay off their loans if they had the money to do so.

I would ask them if they would pay it all off at once. Would they pay some off? Would they pay half off and let their money build back up? I got all kinds of answers from everybody.

I decided to pay off one or two loans at a time. When you repay a loan, the provider sends the original promissory note with a congratulatory letter. I paid off about seven loans in three, maybe four months.

I hesitated regarding the last three loans because I was giving away a lot of money. Plus, it had been a month since I paid off the last ones, and the letter still hadn't arrived. Even though it showed paid on the site, I needed that tangible evidence for my own sake.

This was when the epiphany struck me. Even though I had concluded years ago that school was set up to be modern-day slavery, I didn't see how close and comparable it is to the history of American slavery.

Think about this. I was waiting for my *paper* to show I was *free* of that loan. I needed a piece of paper to confirm my freedom.

During American Slavery, enslaved people couldn't be caught walking around without paperwork showing that they were either free or someone's property.

Sitting there, I couldn't do anything but laugh and frown. Even though I write and talk about a lot of serious stuff, I love to laugh and be goofy. I needed my papers to show that I was free. Woah!

I wrote this for anyone considering going to college. Please consider all your options carefully. You do not; I repeat, you do not want to start your life in debt. And that is what college does, especially for those who go to college without a game plan.

If you are going to go, get some feedback about other peoples' experiences. Ask some people about their coursework. Ask them if they had a job or an internship. Ask them how they balanced them. Ask them if they think their major is worth it. Ask them if they applied for scholarships and grants that lightened the financial load.

These questions will help you to make the best decision when choosing to go to college.

Free Game

This is for all the young people still trying to figure out what they want to do with their lives. I will give you this game and pray that you take heed.

You're 18 and fresh out of high school. Being so young, you may have only worked a few summer jobs or even throughout the year. Either way, you're only 18 years old and probably haven't established any work history or credit.

Let's say you walk into a bank and sit down with an associate hoping to get a $100,000 loan to buy a house and car. You even go to the bank with a well-written plan that shows how clear your vision is.

The associate will listen to your plan. Then, send your application to their loan office, and in a couple of hours or a day, you will likely receive a letter denying your application. One of the reasons for the denial may be that you haven't established long enough credit and work history. (Sidenote to the parents: Add your children to your credit accounts if your credit is good. This will help build their credit and give them a head start.)

Let's say you walk into the same bank and ask the same associate for a $100,000 loan to go to college. She runs your credentials and sees that you need to build your work history and credit. But this time, she comes back and approves you for the loan.

Huh! That should smell fishy to you! Why are you able to get a loan to go to school but not able to get a loan to buy a home? Because they sold you the dream.

They made you believe you would go to school and get a "good" job.

Let's think about that for a second. You are paying to go to school to get a job, to pay for going to school. Don't forget that after six months of graduating, you must pay those student loans back with *interest*!

You might wonder, "What if I don't get a job within six months?" The bank doesn't care and wants more money than it originally lent you. The bank sounds like gangsters to me.

Let's be honest: if you're Black, it may be harder for you to get a job. Because no one ever taught you about nepotism. There are two definitions of nepotism; the only difference is that one uses the word "unfair," and the other doesn't.

Nepotism is practiced among those with power and influence to favor relatives or friends, especially by giving them jobs. Now, let's add "unfair" to the definition. Nepotism is the "unfair" practice among those with power or influence favoring relatives or friends, especially by giving them jobs.

This will sound harsh, and it may seem unfair if you look at it emotionally, but nepotism is the logical thing to do.

For instance, let's say that I own a company. Will I hire a family member or a friend I know I can trust? Or will I hire a random person I have never met before? The person I have never met before only has qualifications on paper (resumes and degrees).

Even if you have more credentials and are better qualified than the boss's cousin, it doesn't matter. It is about survival and making sure that you and yours are good.

These issues aren't only affecting Black youth. Going to college and then having to search for a decent-paying career is hurting everybody. Kids across the country are shoulder-deep in debt. The weight of school debt is depressing and giving millions of kids anxiety.

It's time we stop mindlessly shipping our kids off to school without solid plans for their future. We need to instill entrepreneurship values back into our children. We also need to give them skills that will be profitable forever.

The world will always need carpenters, electricians, farmers, mechanics, plumbers, engineers, doctors, and people with trades and skills. These are the things that will help us progress. No one needs a person with a business degree (I'm taking shots at myself). However, it may help in some instances.

The library is a *free* source of abundant information, and studying there can teach you many things.

I am not trying to deter anyone from going to college. I want people to weigh their options. Is the degree that you want worth the debt? Will going to college help you accomplish your goals? Please sit down and plan it out. Write the pros and the cons, then weigh them.

Call someone who has already gone to school and listen to their story. For the even younger ones reading this and planning to go to college, strive for academic greatness so that you can get scholarships and grants. Having a full ride will significantly reduce your stress after college.

You have to excel in all areas of life, especially in academia. School can be a trap if you don't plan accordingly. That's why this free man is trying to prevent the next man from becoming a slave to debt. Please carefully consider what you read here. Take this game and run with it!

The Love Of Money

Sometimes, you must reevaluate your life and where your heart lies. Recently, I've asked myself if I truly trust in The Most High. As I pondered where and what I've been doing, I realized I was becoming more dependent on money.

It's never what we intend to do, but it sneaks up on us. Before we realize it, we've become more worldly.

I pondered for months whether I should pay off my school loans. I thought about how my bank account balance would be brought down to a number lower than I've seen in years.

I wanted to maintain the comfort money afforded me. At that time, I could've bought and done anything I wanted. Going from abundance to only having means was a scary thought.

Then it hit me: I found solace and comfort in material things. Things that are here today and gone tomorrow. I was caught up.

In Matthew 6:26 it reads, "Look at the birds of the air; they do not sow or reap or store away in barns, and yet your heavenly Father feeds them. Are you not much more valuable than they?" This verse confirms that the Most High will always provide for us.

I had to release the fear of what could happen. A fear that I was making up in my mind. Living in fear is the exact opposite of walking with faith. We should believe that The Most High has given us gifts and abilities to pull us through any situation.

I've been free since I let go of the fear of the unknown. I am no longer caught up in the system. It doesn't weigh on my heart and mind as it once did. This system is designed to keep us tied down with unnecessary burdens.

Sometimes, we get caught up and lose sight of everything that matters. This wasn't written to discourage people from grinding and acquiring wealth because I'm working towards it. But I know how to keep my perspective in order.

There's more to life than money. You should get a lot of it, but make sure that you stay true to yourself. Don't let it change you. Money isn't evil; The Love of money is.

If you find yourself cherishing money more than human life, it's time to reevaluate yourself.

Money is paper with the face of a man you've never met. That man may have owned some of your ancestors, depending on your nationality.

So, I say, get it and use it to better yourself, your family, and your community! Those are the things that matter.

Don't get caught up!

You're A Star

Shine as bright as the North Star. Give people directions without saying a word. Lead by example.

The other day, I went to work out at the field around the corner from my house. When I got there, I set up some cones, hurdles, a ladder, a parachute, and other workout items. After about ten minutes of going in, some kids came out of the school for what looked to be their recess. Oh! The good old days!

About 15 to 20 young teenagers came to the field with a football to play catch.

They were watching me work out. I noticed in their eyes and demeanor that they wanted to join me. I would've let them if a teacher had come around. To me, it is creepy for a grown man to converse with children that he doesn't know. I would've liked for a teacher to come over and look me in the eyes to see the content of my character[11].

One of them finally built up the nerve to ask me if I played football. I told him I didn't play football and liked to work out for my health and fun. Then, I kept working out.

As I was finishing up and stretching, I noticed that some of them were seriously imitating me and my stretch positions. As I said in EXPRESS Yourself[12], life

---

[11] Green, Cliff. "Men of Good Character." *Less Than a Sack of Weed*, 2020, pp 32 - 35
[12] Green, Cliff. "EXPRESS Yourself." *Less Than a Sack of Weed*, 2020, pp 47 - 48

imitates art. I painted a picture of excellence for them to see.

Be the example you seek in others. You can empower people by doing things that are out of the ordinary. The kids may have seen professional athletes do cone and hurdle exercises on TV, but they may have never seen someone do them in person.

I may have lit something in some of those kids' minds. I want them to think they are extraordinary beings. I want them to never stay inside the boxes made for them. I want them to know that they could do the same thing. I want them to do what they love and to love what they do.

Never be scared to shine your light because the world needs to see you shine. Your brightness can illuminate the path for someone stuck in darkness. Please remember that "Somebody's Watching[13]"!

---

[13] Green, Cliff. "Somebody's Watching." *Less Than a Sack of Weed*, 2020, pp 6 - 8

You Scared! You Running!

Before I start, yes, I know that the title is grammatically incorrect. I also know I will get a lot of backlash for saying this, but I'm willing to be the bad guy if it will help others to see. A lot of young Black men are out of their minds. POINT... BLANK... PERIOD!

After running a few errands around the city, I hopped back on the metro to head home. Two young men got on the train a couple of stops before mine. They stood at the doors the whole time.

They both put their backs on the rail while people walked between them to exit the train. When I got off and was already making my way up the steps, one of them said, "You mean to get off here?"

I looked at him, then looked around to see if he was talking to me. Then, I looked at him with a stupid face, my hand on my chest, like me! Then he said, "You scared. You running." Then, the door closed.

Hold on, let's think about this. He said that while he was still standing on the train. Mind you. He had ample opportunity to say something to me when I was standing in front of him, waiting to get off the train. But he didn't. Yet I'm the one who is scared and running. But he's right.

I am running to stay healthy and fit. As I wrote in Somebody's Watching[14], I always run the steps at the

---

14 Green, Cliff. "Somebody's Watching." *Less Than a Sack of Weed*, 2020, pp 6 - 8

same metro station. But do you want to know who I see running with me when I'm out there? I see (insert random White guy's name). I rarely see young Black men running.

For any Black person to ignorantly think anyone or everyone is scared of them because they are Black and from the "hood" is hilarious.

Some of us are training, practicing, and doing everything it takes to become better and stronger. Yet a little ignorant Black man had the nerve to say something to me. I am tired of hood logic.[15]

He might have noticed the frozen food in my bag if he had paid attention. Maybe that is why I looked to be in a rush. Perhaps I wanted to get home and eat.

I don't know why he chose to say something to me; maybe it's because I don't dress like I'm from the Southeast.

His ego let him run off at the lips, thinking he did something to knock me down, but he looked and sounded dumb.

What if I was the one who let my ego control me and jumped back over the rail to confront him? As I stated, I'm out here putting in work, and if you aren't doing the same, you can't see me, nor anybody like me. *Period!*

Let's get to the meat and potatoes. A lot of Black men are scared. They are afraid of and running from reality. The reality is that they are losing. The "white"

[15] Green, Cliff. "Turn Hood Logic into Good Logic." *Less Than a Sack of Weed*, 2020, pp 86 - 87

man, "yellow" man, "purple" man, "red" man, and everybody in between is beating the living crap out of you in every aspect of life.

That's a tough pill to swallow. But you pop pills to get high and escape reality. You play video games and watch TV every day to get away. You drink to drown out your sorrows. You smoke until you forget about yesterday. You get high every day because you are scared to face reality sober.

There is such a thing as recreational smoking, but smoking every day isn't recreational, especially if there isn't anything positive being produced.

I've heard Black men claim to be the biggest gangster. They claim to have never run from anybody or anything. But the truth is, they're scared and running from the reality of life.

You have to be honest with yourself to come to these conclusions. I have talked to many men who admitted to having anxiety about life. We have to find better mechanisms to cope with it. Life is rough sometimes, but it won't get any better if you keep running away from your problems.

To those who would respond by telling me that people are scared of us because we are Black, I'm not going to dive into our genetics because all that means nothing if we aren't doing anything to optimize them. *Period!*

I run miles to optimize mine. Can you say the same?

CommUNITY

The divide between our elders and youth may be beyond repair. The elders don't want anything to do with the youth, and the youth don't want anything to do with the elders. I don't know if there is a way to fix it.

I have iterated the same thing in Less Than a Sack of Weed, but it seems as though the situation has only gotten worse. The community has only separated even further.

The other day, as I was riding the metro home, a bunch of young kids were on the train with me. They were yapping their mouths and saying all kinds of nonsense. Some were loud. Some were talking about being "Lit." Someone said something about how they were twerking. Mind you, these kids were no older than 13, maybe 14.

When they got off the train, an older gentleman said something about how he looked at them and shook his head. He said it as if he could care less about how they acted. He and I shared a few words before I got off the train.

I understand why there is no love between the two. The elders feel it is pointless to talk to today's youth. Who wants to speak to these chaotic kids? Kids who may harm you for no reason.

For instance, a rock was thrown at my back in the story Street Credit is Dead[16]. It almost made me lose hope in our youth. It's wild because helping the youth is one of my passions.

On the flip side, could the youth be so wild because they imitate what they see from the elders? A lot of our elders have dropped the ball. They are the reason why the youth are the way they are.

There's been a war in our community for some time, and the elders lost those battles. They didn't have to let the drugs destroy them. They didn't have to let the TV and society raise their kids. I know they had to work and provide for their families, but not to their detriment.

It's time for us to mend our families and build with one another. One aunt's house is a daycare, this uncle's house is a school, and another runs a business we support. The list of things that we can do will go on and on. These things will help to rebuild the order that our community lacks.

We have to bring back the family structure and support system. We need systems within our families that allow the youth to see how the elders move. They need to be able to talk to their elders and gain wisdom. Today, the so-called elders are getting younger and younger and are more than likely already tainted by this society's ills.

We need to operate as a village again. We can't allow sayings such as "It takes a village" to be sayings

---

[16] Green, Cliff. "Street Credit is Dead." *Less Than a Sack of Weed*, 2020, pp 1 - 5

only. These were values that we lived by. They brought order to our homes and communities. Strong communities make strong neighborhoods, and strong neighborhoods make strong cities.

Business Is Business

F it. I'll be the bad guy. I'm going to go on a whim and say that a lot of Black people DO NOT know how to conduct business.

Of course, not every Black-owned and operated business moves as such. But seeing how some folks operate and conduct business has been somewhat embarrassing.

I've noticed that many Black folks lack the essential components to run a business efficiently. You know, customer service, hospitality, and most importantly, leadership.

"Cliff, why do you keep going hard on Black people? White people have a lot of ills, too." I can't build another man's home when my foundation isn't solid. Once mine is in order, I can work to bring that order to others.

To my young folks with jobs. I understand that you may work in our community and that the people you *serve* may be rude and inconsiderate sometimes, but it's not everyone. You don't have to treat every customer you encounter with an attitude.

I may step into your workplace, and let's say that you are a waitress. If you approach me correctly, I will likely go above and beyond to tip you extra well. It's my way of thanking you for having a bright soul.

Conversely, if you come at me with an attitude, I will try to be the man I am and change your attitude by showing you sincere love. But I won't tip you well if you continue to have a stank face.

I'm using myself as an example, but I know plenty more people would love to tip you. Take this tip from a lesson I learned a while back: kindness always pays off. My hotel room was upgraded not too long ago because I was kind.

To Black business owners, in my opinion- and I could be wrong- I don't see the need to label your business as Black-owned. Business is business. Mark Zuckerberg won't deny you access to Facebook because you're not White. When you run your business well, people will research it and discover who owns it.

Let your excellence speak for itself. Go hard and do what you love. If owning and operating is your thing, operate in a way that brings life and light to you and your company.

If you're working for someone and plan to run your own business one day, shine bright in your current position. Learn what you can and take notes. People are watching you and will help you if they see you have an attitude of greatness.

If you have a product or service for which people exchange money with you to receive that product or service, you, my friend, run a business. I am here to help you run your business efficiently.

Say you have a small restaurant that you operate in the neighborhood you grew up in. A lot of people are showing you love, and some aren't. Things are picking up a little due to word of mouth and a few social media posts.

One of the first things you can do to make your company look more official is to get uniforms or at least wear the same colors. You should not look like you are walking around your house in night clothes. Uniforms look more orderly.

This great-tasting food may have begun in your kitchen, but you took the initiative to turn your cooking abilities into a business. Those abilities can only get you so far. Buy uniforms for you and your employees. The uniforms don't have to be exuberant. They can be cheap khakis and a plain polo shirt you bought at a thrift store. But you should be in uniform.

Have you ever gone to Target and not seen their employees dressed in khakis and red shirts? I'll wait for it. Oh, never! You always see their employees wearing uniforms. That's because uniforms show unity. A business's employees should look like they're playing for the same team.

The same goes for the guys walking through the metro selling body oils. You, my friend, are running a business as well. You should tighten your look and grab a polo and some khakis.

That business professional you just walked by thinks you smell fantastic, but he may not say anything because you look like you're from the streets. You are cutting out a demographic of people whom you can sell to.

Pay attention to how the Mormons come through the neighborhood, selling their religion. They always wear slacks, button-ups, ties, and dress shoes, which makes them look more approachable.

This has nothing to do with European beauty standards but everything to do with commerce and how the world is run. You got into this race; you should be prepared to win. And I am not saying that a suit and tie are a must. Not every businessman or woman needs to dress this way. I am only stating things that can help most businesses.

Let me repeat this: do not call your business a Black business. It is a business, and that's all that it is. I am not saying that we shouldn't support Black-owned and operated businesses because I condone and push for that. I am saying that they do not need to be labeled as Black businesses.

They should just be called businesses. Walmart does not call itself a White business even though a White man founded it. Walmart isn't going to turn you away because you are black, brown, blue, yellow, orange, or white. Walmart wants your green. That is all that matters in the world of business. Walmart also knows the importance of appearance. Therefore, their employees are always dressed in uniform.

This is about how you appear in the eyes of your customers. These stories stem from my experiences in dealing with Black-owned businesses. I often wanted to say something to them but didn't know if it was my place because their attitude and customer service were so bad that I didn't know if my message would be received.

Nonetheless, if you're an entrepreneur working to build an empire, "You're in the big leagues now!" Play the game to win.

Rock Battles

My mom made my sisters, and I read Psalm 91 daily. I know that chapter by heart. It affirms that angels are protecting and guiding us. I know angels are watching over me because I don't know how most young men make it past 18. Seriously, we do the dumbest things as kids. One of the dumbest things that I remember doing growing up was having rock battles.

I wonder who the first kids were who threw rocks at each other for fun. How did that conversation start? "Aye, bro! I thought of the most fun thing ever! We should throw rocks at each other, and whoever gets hit is out!"

The other kid probably picked up a rock and launched it at his boy without a second thought. That's literally how boys operate. My friends and I did whatever seemed fun at the moment. That is one thing about kids: they live in the moment. Something that most of us adults have forgotten how to do.

We threw rocks of all sizes at each other. We launched bricks at each other. We had a clubhouse at the top of this hill in the woods. Climbing the hill was the most convenient way to get to the clubhouse.

At the top of the hill, a tree was set up like a slingshot. We slang bricks and rocks down the hill as people were climbing it.

I know that our ancestors must be watching over us. There is no way that I would be here if they weren't. I don't think that they are looking down at us. They are right here with us, protecting our steps while shaking their heads at our foolishness.

I have too many stories about the foolish things we did growing up. That's how I know I am protected. I have a Destiny with Divinity[17].

There are thousands of people with stories to tell. Unfortunately, most people are caught up in the stories written by Hollywood. It's time to free ourselves from the spells of Holy-wood.

Write your own story. Then have faith that The Most High is guiding you! You made it this far for a reason. Please go to the next level and write about your battles.

---

[17] Green, Cliff. "Destiny with Divinity." *Less Than a Sack of Weed*, 2020, pp 69 - 70

Do You Swallow?

I realize that most people don't know about the dangers of chemicals in their products, especially the chemical known as fluoride. Fluoride is in every major brand of toothpaste. It is also in our tap water. Pause right here and take a minute or two to research the dangers of fluoride.

I will try to give you a quick breakdown of why and how these chemicals harm our health. When you take a liquid medication or supplement, the directions usually tell you to put it under your tongue and swish it around your mouth for maximum absorption into your system.

Think about that and how things easily get absorbed through your mouth. Now think about how millions of people brush their teeth every day and are unknowingly poisoning themselves.

These companies don't even try to hide it from us.

"**Warnings: Keep out of the reach of children under six**. If more than what is used for brushing is swallowed, get medical help or contact the *Poison* Control Center.

So, you're telling me that if I swallow this, I should see a doctor. Geez! I'm using this toothpaste because I thought it would make my mouth healthy.

We have to become more conscious of everything we put into our bodies. You only have one body. It's best to take care of it.

The title of this chapter may have thrown you off. You should know me better than that now, especially if you have read Just Masturbate[18]. I'm here to bring Order Over Chaos.

---

[18] Green, Cliff. "Just Masturbate." *Less Than a Sack of Weed*, 2020, pp 44 - 46

Put It In Writing

I always stress the importance of writing, but I hate it when I don't take my advice. The other day, I had a powerful conversation but didn't write it down. All the knowledge I could've written down and kept in my notes is gone forever.

Don't get me wrong. I have plenty of ideas in all my notebooks, but the idea I had the other day was so powerful that I knew I would go home and write about it. But I didn't, and now I am mad at myself!

I don't like to depend on technology, but sometimes you should use it. If a million-dollar, life-changing, thought-provoking idea pops into your head, don't hesitate to write it in your phone's notes app or send it to yourself via text. It will save you from the despair that I was going through.

I am sure that this has happened to you before as well. It happens to the best of us. Therefore, to prevent future mishaps, do this one simple thing. It will save you from a lot of mental anxiety.

Also, learn to listen intently to other peoples' stories. You may gain something from them. That's why I share my stories. I want to stop someone from making the same mistakes I've made.

Yes Sir! Yes Ma'am!

Should kids address their elders as sir and ma'am? I have been contemplating this question for a while. The good thing I can see is that doing so would raise these kids to respect people.

When we teach them respect early on, they will have fewer problems later. Teaching kids to respect their elders will make them wise beyond their years. Kids who have respect for their elders will likely have respect for everyone else in their lives.

Let me show you how this works. You know in your heart, mind, and soul that you have taught your kid to respect people. You also taught your kid discipline. One day, the teacher calls you and tells you that little Jamal was acting up in class. Your first thought would be that there is no way that your son is acting up because you know you taught him better than that.

The teacher thinks that your child now has behavior problems and wants to put him on medication. A medication that will make him "focus" more. You know he needs a little tune-up from you, and he'll be back on his square.

If you do have an inclination that your child may be acting up in school, instead of believing the teacher's misdiagnosis, do this one day. Randomly show up at your child's school. Ask him aloud in front of his classmates, "What's this I hear about you talking and acting up in Ms. So and So's class?" This will catch him off guard because he didn't expect you to pop up.

Tell the teacher in front of all the students that she can call you anytime and you will be there. Make sure you put some of his friends on the spot as well.

If Jamal respects you as he should because you have instilled values in him since birth, he will no longer act out in class. The fear of not knowing when you may pop up will keep him on his Ps and Qs.

This isn't an outlandish hypothesis. I know because I am little Jamal. I still remember the day that my dad popped up on me. Ever since then, I have been on my best behavior, for the most part, in school.

Try this method out. It works. The proof is in the pudding. My sisters and I were the valedictorians of our classes.

Temple

The human body has been ordained as man's temple throughout most religious and spiritual texts. The word temple can be broken down into temp and le. Temp is the abbreviated version of the word temporary. Temporary is defined as lasting only for a limited period. The le, or the El in Hebrew, is the word for God or deity.

When you combine the two definitions, you create a new meaning for the word temple. Temple can be defined as a temporary position of God, which means while in this body, you should treat it as if it were God's body.

Every day in America, we destroy and show utter disrespect for God. Americans have the highest rate of every illness. We eat the worst type of food. We smoke cigarettes and drink alcohol every day. We fill our minds with poisonous information (TV, music, and media).

Then, we wonder why we were inflicted with so many illnesses and diseases. I know that some things can't be helped. But when you do what you know you shouldn't, that is when consequences arise.

Now that you know this truth, you can hate it, ignore it, or love it and live by it.

Decisions! Decisions!

Monkey See, Monkey Do!

I was riding my bike through D.C. when I stopped at a local park to work out. A few minutes into doing some pull-ups, two young men ran up and started naming the workouts I was doing.

They started to imitate me by doing some pull-ups. They even did some pushups. The one boy grabbed my band and started to do some bicep curls.

A few minutes later, their mother walked over, and we introduced ourselves. She had her daughter with her, who was also intrigued with pull-ups, so she tried to do some. As I interacted with the kids, an older guy came by and started doing some pull-ups.

I said, "That feels good, doesn't it?" He said, "Yeah, but it's been a while since I have done any." I said, "It feels good, though, anyway!" He said, "You're right!"

Children are looking for adults who are doing exciting and cool things. I have said it a thousand times before and will repeat it until I am blue: BE CAREFUL OF WHAT YOU PORTRAY TO THE YOUTH AS COOL!

Please don't complain about the youth's lack of enthusiasm for the outdoors or education, but you spend all your time sitting on the couch. We have to show them by taking the initiative and doing what we want them to do. We have to lead by example.

Think back to when you were a kid. Didn't you imitate people just for fun? Or to annoy that person. The same goes for the children of today. They will imitate you even if you don't know that they are.

Society has conditioned us to have hardened hearts[19]. We have forgotten about how joyful it is to be a child. We have to reevaluate our hearts, minds, souls, and actions.

Never forget that somebody is always watching you!

---

[19] Green, Cliff. "Hardened Hearts." *Less Than a Sack of Weed*, 2020, pp 21 - 24

Lay Down The Law

Men should treat their bodies as if God Almighty lived within them. A diet of fruits, vegetables, herbs, and seeds will help men stand tall and lay down the law.

Before there was a blue pill, men ingested fruits, vegetables, and herbs that boosted their libidos.

Take watermelon, for instance. It's one of the best fruits for our genitals. Watermelon is high in the amino acid citrulline. Citrulline turns into the amino acid arginine. The arginine converts into nitric oxide.

Nitric oxide increases blood flow, which controls the quality and strength of our erections. Men should eat foods that keep their blood flowing optimally.

Who wants to be the guy who ruins the heat of the moment because he can't stand up? Let's say you're out with your wife, and you two have been laughing and flirting all day.

You'll head back to the car, and she's ready to hop in the backseat and get started, but you forgot to pop your blue pill. Your Johnson is limp. You would probably sit there and make every excuse as to why that happened.

You've tried everything possible to get your woman back in the mood, but the moment has passed. The excitement is gone, and the drive back home is a drag. You missed an opportunity to Lay Down the Law.

That story is no bueno. I don't think any man enjoys having to pop a pill to get it popping. Men should act now to prevent a story like that from happening. Eat the foods that give life. Exercise and work out daily. Even if it's just simple things like walking, your overall health affects your man below.

Try to eat fruits with seeds in them. I don't want to steer off-topic, but don't you find it fishy that they are taking the seeds out of the fruits?

In Genesis 1, verses 11 and 12 say:

11 Then God said, "Let the land produce vegetation: seed-bearing plants and trees on the land that bear fruit with seed in it, according to their various kinds." And it was so.

12 The land produced vegetation: plant-bearing seed according to their kinds and trees bearing fruit with seed in it according to their kinds. And God saw that it was good.

As I wrote this, God reminded me that we call our children our seeds, right? When you eat plenty of watermelon, you can plant many seeds and fulfill what the Creator had commanded us to do in the beginning: procreate and multiply.

When you're laying down the law in the bedroom, your woman will listen more intently. Your little head's health coincides with your position in the house. And as I stated in the Preface, the Man is the Head.

Taking care of your temple is a prerequisite to caring for your home.

Clear Conscience

My best friend told me a while back that I needed to quit sitting on all the ideas I had locked up in my mind. He was right! I need to buckle down and focus.
I would hate for my descendants to flip through my notebooks in disbelief at everything I thought of but never brought to light.

If you feel like something you are doing isn't building you up, it's time to reevaluate it. You may do it in your spare time, but sometimes, leisure time can become excessive. Google's definition of leisure is "free time." At this point in my life, I don't feel like I have free time. It's either I am all in or all out.

God gave me gifts that he commanded me to use. God gave us all gifts. It's only right that we share them with the world. Or forever rest in agony.

Nothing hurts more than saying, "I could've done this, or I should've done that!" I don't want to live with that on my conscience, nor should you.

Build Something Tangible

I have been so focused on business ventures lately that my writing has fallen off. It's not that I don't care for writing; I love it. However, writing has moved down on my goal list as I learn about myself and how the world operates.

Though I love it, writing isn't as effective as it once was. It's a sad but harsh reality. Most people don't read and don't choose reading as an everyday luxury.

But most people would like to be successful, not realizing that successful people read daily! They don't understand that everything they follow, from their favorite TV show to religion and laws, has been written and read.

Writers run the world. Even though I am a writer, I don't want to only be a bunch of words on paper. I want my actions to match what I speak. Along with writing, I have been working to build things.

People like to talk about how Black people were/ are the Egyptians and Moors. But why aren't we building pyramids if we're all of that? Where are our present pyramids? It doesn't have to be pyramids per se, but where are our buildings, homes, and businesses? That's where I am right now. I'm building.

I am working to become a living example of excellence. My success is a Black success. I was a Black man the last time I looked in the mirror. There is no need to scream it when you're living it day by day.

I don't want to be another person who writes books, but people can't see anything that looks prosperous in me. That is the sad part. We are in an age of visualization. Everything is for the look. Too many people look successful, but they are broke.

I want to amass wealth that can create wealth and prosperity for everyone else. I am building something tangible.

He Who Hesitates Is Lost

Nobody cares about you as much as you do. There are some people out there who do have your best interest in mind. But they still can't care about you as much as you care about yourself.

Therefore, you should invest in yourself. Do the things that make you better. Purchase the items that will help you develop as a person. Purchase them without hesitation.

We sometimes debate whether to purchase something because the price tag may be steep. Most of the time, that item is worth it. Have you ever wanted a product but let the price tag deter you?

You put it down only to think about it later. Then you go back to the store to pick up the same product, debate it in your mind, and put it back down again. I know I have done this many times. I discovered that it was everything I wanted when I purchased the product.

I do not condone pure consumerism because many people spend their money on foolish items. I am talking about those items that you have envisioned as helpful. You know there will be a good return on your investment, but you were too scared to invest then.

You hesitated. And when you finally return to grab it, it's gone. You end up missing an opportunity. That feeling burns.

Do you work to make money to buy the things that will make you happy and better? Don't let money be the determining factor in how you live and enjoy your life. Work to get it, get a lot of it, but don't hoard it away. Enjoy it. At the same time, make sure that you are leaving something behind for generations to come.

The hesitation comes from doubt and fear. You have nothing to fear. You got it. Invest in yourself! That is one decision that you will never regret. Neither will the people who come behind you.

Have faith in yourself and your God-given gifts. Do you remember when I told you not to waste them? The next chapter will prayerfully give you the push you need to excel at everything you put your mind to.

Success Is Your Only Option

We're supposed to have faith the size of a mustard seed. Do you know how tiny a mustard seed is? With faith as small as a mustard seed, you can accomplish anything.

Have faith in yourself. I know there are times when our faith wavers, when our dreams seem impossible to accomplish, and when we may hesitate to act on them. The hesitation comes from our fear of the "what if?"

What if my idea doesn't work? What if it isn't good enough? What if I can't do it? What if people don't like it? Stop asking yourself doubtful questions!

Start asking yourself about the possibilities. Please don't doubt your God-given abilities because people are waiting for you. We need to see your light shine.

I've learned that every thought of mine is possible. Everything comes from my thoughts. Knowing this has made my "what ifs" limitless. I think big and imagine even bigger. My thoughts have no boundaries.

Never let anything stop you from pursuing your dreams. Have faith in yourself; a little bit goes a long way.

What if success was your only option? What if you believed you could do it? You'll never know until you know. You will be angry at yourself if you allow doubt to stop you from pursuing your dreams and ambitions.

Start asking yourself, "What if I succeed?".
Wording questions differently gives us a new
perspective on our possibilities.

I am telling you to go for everything you deserve.
You can and will succeed because success is your only
option. Believe that!

A Master Of All Trades

It's hard to focus in this day and age. Something is always pulling you this way or another. Well, at least I can speak for myself. I have many interests and sometimes tend to distract myself because of them.

I will be working on this project, but somehow, thoughts of other projects pop into my mind. I caught myself working towards different goals before I completed the initial one. This raises the question: Is a jack of all trades the master of none?

I have accomplished many things thus far and will achieve many more when I give my undivided attention to the task. Being a jack of all trades and a master of one has separate benefits.

If you're only good at one thing, then your value is only quantified by that one thing. It seems you didn't bring that much to the table.

But if you mastered one trade and your neighbor got another trade. Soon, there will be multiple masters.

On the other hand, the jack of all trades is knocking things out left and right and can be called at a moment's notice whenever or wherever they are needed.

How do you become a master of all trades? Master one thing, then move on to the next. Learn how to do something new. Try it, fail at it, then get back up and do it again until you have conquered it.

Explore all of the possibilities that life has to offer. Not only will it make you happier, but it will also make you a brighter person in the eyes of others.

They Will Never Know

They will never know what life is like without cell phones.

They will never know what it feels like to be a completely free human being.

They will never know how to imagine.

They will never know true friendship.

They will never know what life is like without Wi-Fi.

They will never know what not having cable is like.

They will never know real music.

I'm interested in knowing if kids have gone outside as much as they used to before the advent of the cell phone.
There are so many things that the youth are missing out on. I feel incredibly blessed to have come up in the era that I did. I had an adventurous childhood.
There are so many things that *they will never know*. I would like to hear your responses. Please message me on social media, and let's continue this conversation.

What Would You Have Done?

I remember walking home on a side street that leads directly to my house. I approached a house with a dog in the yard. The dog didn't have a leash on, and the house didn't have a fence on the side of the street I was walking on. So, I took a quick left onto the connecting street.

A man in his car rolled down his window as I walked past. He asked me if I made the left because I saw the dog in the yard. I told him that I did. And that the dog didn't look like it had a leash on. He told me that the dog didn't bite and that it would've been cool to walk by it. I told him that I didn't know about that. That dog is enormous. We laughed, and then I kept moving.

As I continued to walk down the street, I kept my eye on the dog. I noticed that the dog paced left and right. Then, he ran around the fence in my direction. So, I ran and jumped on the car that was closest to me.

Coincidentally, the dog's owner owned the car I jumped on. I dented the roof as I jumped on it. The dog ran down the street, and the lady chased him. She came back and was angry that I put a dent in her car.

She irately told me that the dog didn't bite and that she had just got the car. I told her that I didn't know that dog and whether or not it bites.

I tried to reason with her. My initial reaction was to pay for the damage. So, I gave her my name and phone number. But as I conferred with other people, they all reasoned with me that the damage wasn't my fault. She should've had her dog on a leash. She should've trained the dog not to leave the yard.

As I walked away, I heard her say something about having someone beat me up, but when I turned around, she was already in the house.

My boy pointed out that the situation would've been different if I were a Caucasian man. She would've more than likely apologized to me and shown humility.

Instead, she popped off at me since I am Black. She showed more sympathy for an inanimate object than another human's well-being. The dent in the car could've easily been fixed, but scars to the flesh don't heal as well.

Why is there so much hate among people? Was I wrong for jumping on the roof of the car? What would you have done?

cRAP Music

A lot of cRAP music is destroying our youth. In one verse, a rapper will talk about how he lost some homies to the streets. Then, he will turn around and glorify the streets in the next verse. It's time for a change. I need these "artists" to see the problem in their message.

I have heard rappers argue that movies show way more violence, so why isn't anyone targeting movies? It's true. Movies display a lot of violence and subliminal messages. But no one goes around humming movie scripts all day. You will catch people randomly singing music, though. That is because music is powerful.

Try this one day. Ask a kid to do a simple math or algebra question and watch him sit there and struggle for his dear life. Then, ask him to sing the lyrics to a song. I bet he sings the song without hesitation.

Everything manifests from our thoughts, and our thoughts shape our reality. Chairs didn't always exist until someone came up with the idea after being tired of standing.

Sitting comfortably consumed their thinking until they designed what we know as a chair. Their thought manifested into a chair. Of course, they had to work to bring the chair into reality, but the chair started from a single idea. I used a chair as an example, but that goes for every invention we use in this physical world.

The Black community is chaotic. This is because our thoughts are aligned with death and destruction. These are the things that most, not all, cRAP is about. Someone will always give the counter-argument saying, "Well, I listen to cRAP, and I am doing ok." But "ok" isn't good enough. I am speaking about things that will have us doing GREAT!

Every other culture on this planet understands the power of thought. It is about time that we learn to use our thoughts accordingly. Quit listening to cRAP that pollutes your mind. Especially while driving around with your kids in the car. Kids absorb everything they hear. Don't pollute their minds before they can explore them.

When you get a chance, read "As a Man Thinketh" by James Allen.

I pray that this message moves you to clear your thoughts. Your thoughts control your destiny. Don't let cRAP music deter you from your destination.

I write this with love and hope!

The Solutions

I've realized that people don't want it. It's easier to cry about the situation than to do something about it.

It's so clear to see now. You can have all of the solutions. You can have the game plan and be ready to bring the solutions.

But solutions take hard work. They won't show themselves overnight. They will take time, dedication, discipline, and vision.

Did you catch that? It takes vision to bring about solutions. You have to see further than you currently are. You must be open-minded and humble to see that someone's vision may be more precise than yours. In our humility, great work will blossom.

Humility will allow us to accept that we're not always the One. Other people may have a vision, too. When we see that they have it, humility and wisdom will tell us to get behind and support this person's vision because we will understand that it's for the bigger picture.

I pray that this chapter has softened your heart. I pray that when you meet people with a clear vision, you know when to follow because you are someone who brings about solutions instead of someone who only talks about the problem.

The solutions are all around us. We must be humble enough to see and work towards them.

Nothing in life that is worth something comes easily. It's time to work if we want these problems solved! Are you ready to get your hands dirty?

The Key To Success

Organization is a major key to success. It's easy to see the difference between a well-put-together person and an untidy person. It shows in how they dress and carry themself.

A well-organized person's aura looks bright. Their head is up, and their eyes are straight while walking. They're focused on their objective. Their clothes fit sharply. An organized person looks like they have somewhere important to be.

I can't speak about Organization[20] without speaking about cleanliness. What did Money Mitch say? *"Cleanliness is next to godliness."* An organized person is always clean and looks godly.

Most of us work for a corporation or company. We call companies and corporations *organizations*. To run a company properly, you need organization and order.

To succeed in life, you need organization and order. Some people may have never witnessed order in their household. I suggest you read the Bible, and it will give you direction.

Delete your social media apps until your thoughts are your thoughts. Right now is not the time to let outside influences infiltrate your mind. Regain control of your mind.

---

[20] Green, Cliff. "ORGANIZATION." *Less Than a Sack of Weed*, 2020, pp 91 - 92

You have a vision of what you want to accomplish. Write down your vision, make your plan, and execute your plan.

The supreme key to success is to plan for it! Having a plan puts your steps in order.

Change Your Routine

A few years back, my Uncle Kevin told me to change my routine by hopping out of bed on the other side. The following day, I took his advice, changed my routine, and was offered a job later that day. I chose to try something different, and it worked.

We should strive to change our monotonous habits. Many of our habits keep us stuck in a cycle we will never grow from. If the purpose of life is to be the best we can be, the best has endless possibilities when we're willing to explore them. Don't be afraid of change.

Start with something simple. When you wake up tomorrow, hop out of bed on the other side. Do something to break a habit of yours. Brush your teeth with your non-dominant hand. Do something out of the ordinary.

A change of routine may take you places.

Push Yourself

Am I crazy? I like to stare in the mirror and motivate myself. I am hard on myself when I do something I know I am not supposed to do. No, I am not stressed. I'm lining myself up.

A friend once said that I shouldn't be so hard on myself. But if I'm not hard on myself, then who would be?

I wouldn't accomplish much if I were easy on myself. I like to keep myself on my toes. I take responsibility for my actions or lack thereof. I hold myself accountable for everything.

I love myself to the fullest. I know my capabilities and what I can accomplish. I work hard not to let myself, God, my family, or my friends down.

Go Hard or Die Easy[21] isn't just a motto I live by. It's a lifestyle.

How do you push yourself?

---

[21] Green, Cliff. "Go Hard or Die Easy." *Less Than a Sack of Weed*, 2020, pp 39 – 41

Reward Greatness

I remember riding to the store in my dad's truck. As I entered the parking lot, I saw two young men walking behind their mom.

One of the young men walked right in front of the truck without looking. The other started to walk, noticed I was coming, stopped, and put his arm out to stop his brother from walking.

I stopped the truck and waved them on. They waved back and then ran ahead to catch up to their mom.

I was so impressed with the young man that I had to say something to him. After entering the store, I found them and asked them which one had stopped when they saw the truck. I couldn't tell who was who because they were twins. Their names were Jamere and Jamelle. Jamere stopped for me.

I introduced myself to them and their mother as Mr. Cliff. Then I told Jamere that it was brilliant of him to stop and pay attention to the truck. I complimented him on his intellect and told his brother that he should follow his lead.

Not to say that his brother wasn't thoughtful, but in that moment, Jamere outshined him. Jamere went on to tell me that his father always told him to pay attention to his surroundings. Shout out to the fathers who instill valuable lessons in their children.

I offered to buy them anything they wanted in the store, including small Nerf guns. They were both very appreciative, and so was their mother.

They both told me they wanted to have Lambos in the future. I told them they should keep their grades up and grind for what they want. Anything is possible when you're focused.

I asked them if they had raked leaves and shoveled snow. I was giving them ideas of hustles they could start early. They were only about nine or ten years old.

We should compliment kids when they're doing great. Let's reward them for their work.

Prayerfully, I planted something inside those two that will continue growing as they age. I am sure that if our kids received more love from more places, we would see a positive change in them.

The world tries to teach them that they will reap the rewards by being ignorant and acting foolish. That couldn't be any further from the truth. Let's change the narrative while we change our youths' mindset. Let's motivate them to be great.

The Power Of Fatherhood – Clifford Green

Let me tell you about the power of fatherhood. As I stated in the preface, men bring order. It is a man's job to bring order to his household. That was not said to take anything from the women's role in the house.

My sisters and I graduated at the top of our classes, and I vividly remember the incident that got me there. I was thirteen in the eighth grade, cutting up in class, thinking I was making some noise.

Unbeknownst to me, the teacher had called my father and told him to come to her class as soon as possible. I was joking and causing chaos in class while the teacher was trying to teach. My heart dropped when my dad walked into the room.

How scared would you have been? Well, I was shaking in my boots. Everybody in the community knows my dad and how he gets down. Everyone knows he's not for the nonsense, either. The fear and embarrassment I had on my face were enough to make my friends scared, too.

The fear of not knowing when my pops would pop up led me to stay on my Ps and Qs while in school. I love my mom, and she has gracefully guided me in life, but I wouldn't have been scared if she had shown up. I would've thought she might've been bringing me lunch, as she often so lovingly did.

My dad subtly made me realize years later that I could write. As a teen, I didn't think I could write. Look at me now; I am three books in.

My dad wrote my valedictorian speech, which has become more prophetic with time. I thank the Most High for inspiring him to write a compelling speech. The only thing I did was read it aloud, extremely nervous in front of a crowd. The speech can be read below:

Good evening, parents, teachers, faculty, Mr. Tindal, school board members, Mr. Perrin, fellow students, and graduates.

For the class of 2004, the odds were stacked against us. We stand here as proof with the grace of God that all things are possible under his guidance.

As I look out amongst all of you, I see an unknown future for you. A future in which you have a choice to make. Will you stay the course and fill your mind with the desire to do things that will better this world and your life? Or will you succumb to the system and be another statistic of your environment?

We, the class of 2004, have chosen the former. We have lived on both sides of the road. We have met the odds and fulfilled them.

Some of us may be content with a high school diploma, but some, like myself, choose to go to the next level. My heart desires that those we leave behind will be inspired by the class of 2004. The education is here. All you need is the determination to excel.

Be your best and try not to fall along the road. To be passed by as an empty chair, fill the chair, raise those hands, ask them questions, and seek the knowledge before you.

Be as we were before, graduates of 2004. Reach out and take what is yours. We have the great Martin Luther King, the inspiring Malcolm X, and the great writings of Langston Hughes, James Baldwin, and Alice Walker.

We have the performing arts of Harry Bellefonte, Sidney Poitier, and Lena Horne. They have come before you and laid down the crown. All you need to do is put it on.

There are so many inspiring African-American role models that I can't even begin to list them all. But I must tell you, we are a race that engineered the beginning of civilization. We came from nations of kings and queens. My heart is wretched with what I see outside.

So many of my peers have fallen for the easy way out: the fast money, the drugs, the cars. But we who stayed the course chose the path of our ancestors.

We shall carry on the legacy of what it means to come from the great land of our ancestors: engineers, doctors, chemists, kings, queens, performing artists, writers, and politicians—the true pioneers of civilization.

This is the road I chose with so much behind me, such greatness. I hope to bring honor to my parents, school, and, most importantly, God Almighty. The great I am, the first, the last, the Alpha, the Omega, to him be the Glory.

Thank you, Amen.

I pray more fathers take an active role in their children's lives. When men act as leaders and disciplinaries, order will return to this world.

I thank my father, Clifford Green, for guiding me through life. The power of fatherhood is why I choose Order Over Chaos.

P.S. If you thought my speech was on point, wait until you read what Stephanie and Victoria wrote.

Thank YOU!!!

Thank you for buying and reading Order Over Chaos. May your days be filled with peace, love, joy, order, and prosperity!

Did you love this book? If so, please take a moment to write a review. Your review will help this book reach more people.

Please stay in the loop by following me **@Cliffgr33n** on social media & by going to **www.cliffgr33n.com.**

Check out Go Hard Or Die Easy ® apparel at **www.gohardordieeasy.com**

**ORDER
OVER
CHAOS**

www.ingramcontent.com/pod-product-compliance
Lightning Source LLC
Chambersburg PA
CBHW070128030426
42335CB00016B/2298